for my boys...

beauty is within grasp

Robbie Burns

We are a family of collectors.

Not of fine art (though that would be
nice too) but of the more mundane conkers,
pebbles, feathers, fossils and shells.
My boys became collectors the very moment
they were able to put things in their
pockets. We have an old glass fronted
cupboard in our hall filled to the brim
with treasures - the boys call it the
Curiosity Cabinet and if you visit one
day and are very lucky they will sit you
down in front of it and share the stories
of how they came by such interesting things.

So, you see it was really only a matter
of time before our nature collecting
became a book, this book, which almost
wrote itself.

Turns out I've been collecting ideas
for years too.

Janet x

warms the land

Spring is my very favourite season.

It's just bursting with promise isn't it?
And you can't help but be cheerful when the
days are growing steadily longer and warmer,
and all the colours start coming back too.
Everyone and everything has energy again.
Spring is simply a joy.

So, this chapter celebrates all the things
I love most about the Spring: primroses and
forget-me-not's, bunnies and birds. I hope
the projects help you welcome and celebrate
this lovely season.

After the long, grey winter there comes the very welcome sight of Spring flowers. Each friendly little Bluebell and Primrose tells you that warmer, gentler days are just around the corner.

And so, here are some of my favourite Spring flowers on one charming quilt. I'm rather pleased with this one (if I do say so myself!)

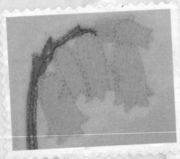

Finished quilt measures 36 x 45 inches

JOYS OF SPRING QUILT.

REQUIREMENTS:

Fabrics for 20 plain
5 x 9½ inch blocks

Calico for 20 appliqué
5 x 9½ inch blocks

Fabrics for the flower appliqué:
¼ yard of each colour,
½ yard green

Fusible web: 1 yard

Binding: ½ yard

Wadding and backing fabric:
39 x 48 inches

Cream thread for piecing and quilting

Polyester threads to match flowers
for free machine drawing

INSTRUCTIONS:

1. **PREPARE:** Wash and press fabric.
   Cut twenty 5 x 9½ inch rectangles in a variety of fabrics. Cut twenty 5 x 9½ inch rectangles in calico.

2. **APPLIQUÉ:** Make five of each flower. Arrange each flower carefully in the centre of the calico rectangles. See 'How do I?' chapter for tutorial.

3. **FREE MOTION STITCHING:** Place stabiliser behind the appliqué blocks before free motion stitching in matching threads (see 'How do I?' chapter for tutorial). Press.

4. **PIECE:** Alternating fabric and appliqué blocks, piece five rows of eight blocks. The first row starts with a fabric block. Piece the rows together. Press.

5. **MARK UP QUILTING:** Using a removable fabric pen trace the quilting template.

6. **LAYER UP:** Add wadding and backing fabric.

7. **QUILT:** I hand quilted around the flowers and a diagonal cross with a circle of feathers in the middle of each fabric block.

8. **MAKE BINDING:** Cut 3 inch wide strips for double fold continuous binding. Stitch in place.

9. Show your quilt off to everyone – and never point out your mistakes!

pieces
of
song

Finished cushion: $11^1/_2$ x $11^1/_2$ inches

I really like Blackbirds with their glossy black feathers and striking yellow beak. And I love to hear them sing. My friend told me their song is at its best just after the rain has stopped, which only makes me like them more.

PIECES OF SONG CUSHION.

REQUIREMENTS:
12 x 12 inches fabric for cushion front
Two 12 x 9 inches fabric for cushion envelope back
Bondaweb
Appliqué fabric
12 x 12 inches thin wadding
Sewing, embroidery and quilting threads

INSTRUCTIONS:

1. **PREPARE THE FABRIC:** Wash and press your fabric.

2. **APPLIQUÉ:** Trace the blackbird onto Bondaweb. Arrange carefully to the left hand side of the fabric. Press. See 'How do I?' chapter for tutorial.

3. **TRACE** words and quilting templates onto fabric.

4. **ADD WADDING** behind the fabric.

5. **FREE MOTION STITCHING:** Add wings and details to your Blackbird by free motion stitching the appliqué (see 'How do I?' chapter for tutorial). Press.

6. **USE A HOOP:** Place your fabric in the hoop making sure it is taut enough to make a satisfying little 'pop' when you pull the needle through, but be sure not to stretch it out of shape.

7. **BEGIN STITCHING THE WORDS:** Sew with three strands of embroidery silk and back or split stitch.

8. **QUILT:** Hand quilt the feather wreath templates with small stitches. Remove template lines.

9. **MAKE CUSHION:** Mine has an envelope back.

10. **SHOW OFF!** And never, ever point out your mistakes!

Finished size: 12 x 5 inches

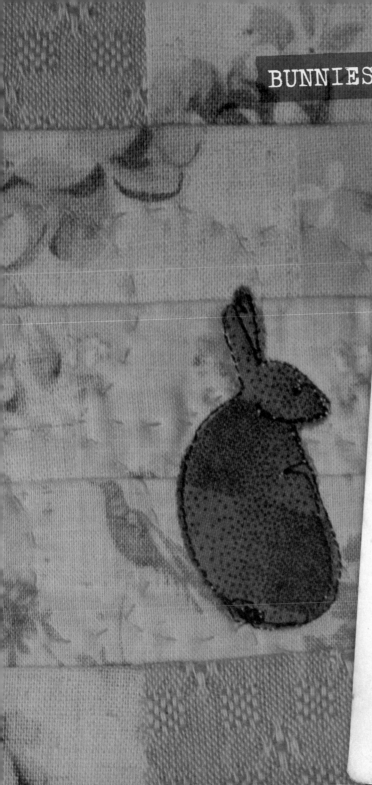

BUNNIES APPLIQUÉ PICTURE.

This little picture was inspired by the rabbits I enjoy seeing in the fields as I whizz past in the train or car. I never seem to see them at any other times, which is probably because I'm with a dog and two boys who give any wildlife ample warning to run away and hide long before we can catch a glimpse!

And of course, children (big and small alike) will be looking forward to the best bunny of all- the Easter Bunny.

REQUIREMENTS:

$1\frac{1}{2}$ inch wide scraps fabric for background

Brown fabric and Bondaweb for Bunnies

Wadding and backing fabric: $12\frac{1}{2}$ x $5\frac{1}{2}$ inches

INSTRUCTIONS:

1. **PREPARE THE FABRIC.** Wash and press your fabric.

2. **CUT FABRIC:** Cut your background fabric into $1\frac{1}{2}$ inch wide strips of any length.

3. **PIECE BACKGROUND:** Chain-piece your strips together to form a $12\frac{1}{2}$ x $5\frac{1}{2}$ inch background.

4. **APPLIQUÉ:** Trace the bunnies onto Bondaweb. Arrange them carefully on your background. Press. See 'How do I?' chapter for tutorial.

5. **ADD WADDING** behind the fabric.

6. **FREE MOTION STITCHING:** Free motion stitch the appliqué (see 'How do I?' chapter for tutorial). Press.

7. **ADD BACKING FABRIC:** With right sides together place backing fabric on top of your appliqué picture. Sew round leaving an opening for turning. Trim corners. Slip stitch the opening closed.

8. **SHOW OFF!** And never, ever point out your mistakes!

TEMPLATES – see pages 72 & 73

Have you tried eating nettles?
You should- they're quite
delicious whizzed up in a soup.
And they're free too. Although
you might be wise not to mention
the 'special' ingredient until
everyone has agreed they like it!

NETTLE SOUP...

INGREDIENTS:

FORAGING KIT: Rubber gloves, bag, scissors
1 medium onion finely sliced
1 pint of vegetable stock
1 large potato, diced and boiled
Black pepper
Crème fraiche
1 large carrier bag of fresh nettle tops
Butter

METHOD:

Melt the butter slowly then add the onion,
cooking over a gentle heat until it is
soft and translucent. Add the vegetable
stock and heat until it gently simmers.
Skim any scum off the surface. Add the
nettles and simmer for about 5 minutes.
Add the potato and keep cooking for
5 more minutes. Take off the heat and
season. Whizz in a food processor.
Stir in some crème fraiche and serve!

LIGHTNING PROTECTION.

Did you know that nettles make the
most beautiful soft white cloth? And
if turning those prickly leaves into
cloth isn't magic enough, it is said
to bestow courage on the wearer too.

They also say that carrying a sprig
or two of nettles in your pocket will
protect you from lightning. So, I
couldn't resist embroidering a bunch
of nettles onto a little pocket for my
cardigan- and it must work, because
I've never been struck by lightning!

REQUIREMENTS:

5 x 5 inches fabric for front
and back of pocket
Sewing and embroidery threads

INSTRUCTIONS:

1. **PREPARE THE FABRIC:**
   Wash and press your fabric.

2. **TRACE** nettle onto front fabric.

3. **BEGIN STITCHING THE OUTLINE:**
   Sew with three strands of embroidery
   silk and a back stitch or split stitch.

4. **NOW STITCH THE DETAILS:** Changing the
   thickness of your embroidery silk
   (from three to two strands) will add
   depth and texture to your embroidery.

5. **MAKE POCKET:** With right sides together
   place backing fabric on top of your
   embroidery. Sew round leaving an opening
   for turning. Clip curves. Slip stitch
   the opening closed. Top stitch to keep
   the layers together.

6. **SEW ON CARDIGAN:** With a small
   slipstitch, sew your pocket in place.

LITTLE IDEAS....

Tulip embroidery on vintage fabrics

Spring flowers as a bouquet on a cushion

Shimmering heat

I'll whisper this...

Summer is not my
favourite season.

Still, there are plenty of things
I do enjoy about the season; the
long days, lazy picnics and the
ease the gentler weather brings.
The projects in this chapter
should help you make the most
of our fleeting sunshine.
So get sewing whilst it
rains and hope we have a
balmy English summer.full
of strawberries and butterflies
and picnics to look forward to.

BUTTERFLIES & BUGS QUILT.

I can't tell you how much fun it was to stitch the ants and spiders into this innocent looking quilt. Don't tell anyone the bugs are there, simply wait for them to be found!

Your quilt will, of course, look different to mine but butterflies can flutter anywhere and you should have no trouble hiding a few ants amongst the embroidery. This is such a fun project- I highly recommend you make it!

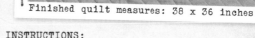

Finished quilt measures: 38 x 36 inches

REQUIREMENTS:

Vintage tablecloth

Fabric scraps for the butterflies and bugs appliqué

Fusible web: ½ yard

Binding: ¼ yard

Wadding and backing fabric, several inches larger than the tablecloth

Cream thread for hand quilting

Grey polyester thread for free machine drawing

INSTRUCTIONS:

1. **PREPARE:** Wash and press fabric. You can soak your tablecloth in baby sterilising fluid to remove any marks. Cut hems off the tablecloth. Cut backing fabric and wadding to size.

2. **APPLIQUÉ:** Make as many butterflies and bugs as you like. See 'How do I?' chapter for tutorial.

3. **FREE MOTION STITCHING:** Place stabiliser behind the appliqué before free motion stitching in grey thread (see 'How do I?' chapter for tutorial). Press.

4. **EMBROIDER:** I hand stitched the spider legs with long back stitches in sewing thread.

5. **MARK UP QUILTING:** Using a removable fabric pen draw diagonal lines across the quilt 1½ inches apart.

6. **LAYER UP:** Add wadding and backing fabric.

7. **QUILT:** I hand quilted in a cream thread.

8. **MAKE BINDING:** Cut 3 inch wide strips to make a double fold continuous binding. Stitch in place.

9. **SHOW YOUR QUILT OFF TO EVERYONE -** and never point out your mistakes!

A LITTLE IDEA...

Why butterfly?
I'd have called it a flutter-by, wouldn't you?

I love coming out of the hot sun into the cool shade, don't you? I've been collecting shadows in my sketchbook for a while now and suddenly knew what I wanted to do with them. I haven't included any templates because I want you to go and collect your own shadows!

SHADOWS WALL HANGING.

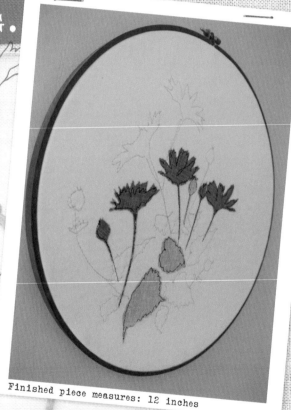

Finished piece measures: 12 inches

REQUIREMENTS:
12 inch embroidery hoop
Grey paint
Grey fabric for appliqué
Background fabric
15 inch square thin wadding

INSTRUCTIONS:

1. **COLLECT YOUR SHADOWS:** Choose a hot day and go into the garden with a pencil and a big piece of paper. Let the flowers cast shadows on the paper and draw round them.

2. **PREPARE FABRIC:** Cut backing fabric to size. Select fabric for the shadows. Trace the background shadows you wish to stitch onto the fabric.

3. **ADD WADDING.**

4. **FREE MOTION STITCHING:** Set your machine for free machine stitching and draw the shadows. Remove the tracing lines.

5. **APPLIQUÉ:** Trace another set of shadows onto Bondaweb and appliqué in place. I used the front and back of the same grey fabric to achieve the shading. See 'How do I?' chapter for tutorial.

6. **FRAME:** I painted my embroidery hoop in a deep grey. Stretch your finished cloth in the hoop and tighten securely. Trim excess fabric, leaving the fabric longer where the screw is. Pull this extra fabric taut and glue to the hoop so it looks neat.

The boys love to collect and study bugs.
They found out that Water Boatmen bite last
summer! I'm hoping this little collectors'
notebook set will encourage them to record
their amazing discoveries.

COLLECTORS NOTES.

REQUIREMENTS:
13 x 7 inch piece blanket or felt
Red thread
Scrap paper
Brown envelope
Safety pin or badge pin

INSTRUCTIONS:

1. **PREPARE THE FABRIC:** Cut blanket to size.
   Draw round a side plate on one 7 inch end to
   create a curve. The curved flap is 3 inches deep.

2. **STITCH CASE:** Fold up the bottom 5 inches and pin
   in place. Stitch all round, this creates the case
   and topstitches the curved flap at the same time.

3. **CUT PAPER:** Cut scrap paper to size: 6 x 5 inches.
   I made 12 sheets. Cut brown envelope for cover:
   $6\frac{1}{2}$ x 5 inches. Fold all paper in half.

4. **SEW NOTEBOOK:** Stitch through all the paper along
   the fold. Tie threads at each end to secure.

A LITTLE IDEA...

Draw a creepy
crawly on your
sewing machine and
wear it with pride!

They say that fresh air is the best
seasoning, so if you make a few of
these little picnic bags, you can
just throw together some sandwiches
and get outdoors for a tastier lunch.

Finished bag measures: 8½ x 8½ inches

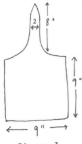
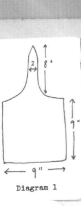

Diagram 1

PICNIC BAG.

REQUIREMENTS:
Fabric for bag and lining
½ yard each

INSTRUCTIONS:

1. **PREPARE FABRICS:**
   Cut to size as shown
   in diagram 1, drawing
   curves between the top
   of the bag and the
   long handles. Shape the
   end of the handles too. Cut two
   in main fabric and two in lining.

Diagram 2

2. **STITCH SIDES:** Stitch the main fabric
   pieces with right sides together.
   Repeat for lining. See diagram 2.

3. **STITCH BOTTOM:** Open out the pieces
   and press seams open. The seams are
   now in the centre of the bag. Stitch
   across the bottom of the pieces, leaving
   a 3 inch opening in the centre of the
   lining for turning later. See diagram 3.

Diagram 3

4. **STITCH CORNERS:** Open out the bottom
   of the bags and measure 1 inch in
   from corner point. Stitch across.
   Trim excess fabric away. See diagram 4.

5. **STITCH BAG:** Place one bag inside
   the other with right side together.
   Pin in place. Stitch all round.
   Clip curves. Turn and press.

6. **TOPSTITCH:** Topstitch all round and press.

7. **ENJOY:** Now take your bag on a picnic!

Diagram 4

Protect your
drinks from the
less welcome
picnic guests...

A LITTLE IDEA...

LITTLE IDEA...

Table runner

I had intended to appliqué some pretty butterflies on this table runner, but just couldn't resist adding a line of busy ants instead.

wisps of mist

I really love the Autumn with its' misty
mornings, cool breezes and rich leafy colours.
I know the nights are slowly drawing in and
the year is growing old; but I always feel
Autumn brings a fresh start. Must be all
those years in education!

It was a pleasure to gather up all
my warm and richly coloured fabrics
and make the projects for this chapter.
I was, of course, inspired by the
changing trees and their delightful
leaves and seeds. How could you not be?

My boys love trees and spend most of their time climbing and sitting in them when we are out and about. And I spend as much time nervously looking up at them. So, I really couldn't have an Autumn chapter without a tree quilt. I didn't sew a boy in a tree, but I probably should have - I rarely see one without a boy in it.

TREES QUILT

Finished quilt measures 40 x 40 inches

REQUIREMENTS:

Fabric for 20½ inch central square, 1 tea stained calico

Fabric for appliqué trees

Fabrics for the 10½ inch wide x 124 inches long borders

Fusible web: ¼ yard

Binding: ½ yard

Wadding and backing fabric: 44 x 44 inches

Wool embroidery thread

TEMPLATES - see page 63-66

INSTRUCTIONS:

1. **PREPARE:** Wash and press all the fabric.

2. **CUT FABRIC:** Cut 20½ inch centre square. Cut 10½ inch x any width strips of fabric for the borders. You need 124 inches minimum.

3. **APPLIQUÉ:** Trace the 4 trees and their seeds and leaves. Arrange each of them carefully on the central square. Press. See 'How do I?' chapter for tutorial.

4. **FREE MOTION STITCHING:** Place stabiliser behind the appliqué before free motion stitching the appliqué (see 'How do I?' chapter for tutorial).

5. **EMBROIDER:** Trace the tree names and embroider with split stitch.

6. **CHAIN PIECE:** Sew fabrics together to form border.

7. **SEW BORDERS:** Sew border fabric to the top and bottom and then each side of the centre square. Trimming to size as you go.

8. **LAYER UP:** Add wadding and backing fabric.

9. **QUILT:** I hand tied the centre square and then machine quilted round it in squares.

10. **MAKE BINDING:** Cut 3 inch wide strips for double fold continuous binding. Stitch in place.

11. **SHOW YOUR QUILT OFF TO EVERYONE** - and never point out your mistakes!

every leaf
speaks bliss
to me
fluttering from the
autumn tree

Finished cushion measures 16 inches

For this cushion I embroidered
a couple of lines from the poem
'Fall, Leaves, Fall' onto some
beautiful indigo linen. So, thank
you Emily Brontë for the inspiration
and your charming words.

REQUIREMENTS:

17 x 17 inches fabric for
cushion front

Two 17 x 12 inches fabric
for cushion envelope back

Embroidery wool

Embroidery hoop

INSTRUCTIONS:

1. **PREPARE THE FABRIC:** Wash and press your
   fabric. Cut to size.

2. **TRACE WORDS AND LEAF TEMPLATES ONTO FABRIC:**
   If your fabric is dark, trace templates onto
   a removable paper and stitch through that.
   I placed my words very high and to the right
   side as you can see.

3. **USE A HOOP:** Place your fabric in the hoop making
   sure it is taut enough to make a satisfying
   little 'pop' when you pull the needle through,
   but be sure not to stretch it out of shape.

4. **BEGIN STITCHING:** Sew with a back stitch or
   split stitch.

5. **MAKE CUSHION:** Sew with a $\frac{1}{2}$ inch seam
   allowance. Mine has an envelope back.

6. **SHOW OFF!** Show everyone your embroidery
   and never, ever point out your mistakes!

The foxes are here because of their lovely colouring and their shapely tail. I could have chosen squirrels for much the same reasons, but to be honest I found foxes easier to draw!

REQUIREMENTS:

17 x 17 inches fabric
e.g. tweed for cushion front

Two 17 x 12 inches fabric
for cushion envelope back

17 x 17 inches thin wadding

Sewing and quilting threads

INSTRUCTIONS:

1. **PREPARE THE FABRIC:** Wash and press your fabric. Cut to size.

2. **APPLIQUÉ:** Trace the two foxes. Arrange them carefully on the cushion front. Press. See 'How do I?' chapter for tutorial.

3. **FREE MOTION STITCHING:** Place stabiliser behind the appliqué before free motion stitching the appliqué (see 'How do I?' chapter for tutorial).

4. **TRACE QUILTING TEMPLATE ONTO FABRIC.** If your fabric is dark, trace quilting lines onto a removable paper and stitch through that.

5. **QUILT.** Add wadding behind the fabric. Hand quilt the feather templates with small stitches. Remove template lines.

6. **MAKE CUSHION:** Mine has an envelope back.

7. **SHOW OFF!** Show everyone your cushion and never, ever point out your mistakes!

TEMPLATES – see page 79

TWO FOX CUSHION.

Finished cushion measures 16 inches

GRASS EMBROIDERY.

TEMPLATES - see page 69

One day we had a picnic and ate watching the wind blowing the long grassy crops around and the sun catching them as they swayed. It was beautiful. When I got home I stitched this grass embroidery. It's nowhere near as lovely as what inspired it though.

Finished size: 10½ x 7 inches

REQUIREMENTS:

Fabric for front and back
11 x 7½ inches

Wadding 10½ x 7 inches

Embroidery silks:
2 shades of green

Tea

INSTRUCTIONS:

1. **PREPARE THE FABRIC:** Cut fabric for the front and back to size.

2. **TRACE GRASS TEMPLATE ONTO FABRIC.**

3. **ADD WADDING:** This will hide your thread ends and adds texture.

4. **BEGIN STITCHING THE OUTLINE:** Sew the stems and leaves with three strands of embroidery silk in split stitch.

5. **NOW STITCH THE DETAILS:** Embroider the 'ears' with two strands of embroidery silk.

6. **BE BRAVE:** When the embroidery was finished I very boldly dyed it in tea. Iron whilst wet to get the maximum difference in tone.

7. **SEW BACKING:** Sew all round with right sides together leaving an opening for turning. Turn right side out. Slip stitch opening closed. Press to neaten.

8. **FRAME:** Attach to mount board using glue dots and frame.

A LITTLE IDEA...

Gathered circles of tweed and buttons have made my coat pretty special...

SHAWL.

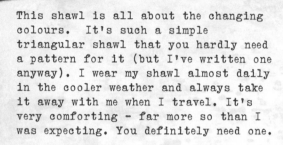

This shawl is all about the changing colours. It's such a simple triangular shawl that you hardly need a pattern for it (but I've written one anyway). I wear my shawl almost daily in the cooler weather and always take it away with me when I travel. It's very comforting - far more so than I was expecting. You definitely need one.

REQUIREMENTS:

You can knit this shawl in any yarn:

I used 200 grams of self-striping aran weight yarn

Needles to match yarn weight

INSTRUCTIONS:

You can knit this triangular shawl any size you like, simply increase the stitches for half your yarn and decrease for the other half. Garter stitch throughout.

CAST ON: Cast on 5 stitches

<u>TO INCREASE:</u>

1ST ROW: knit to end

2ND AND EVERY ALT ROW: knit to last 2 stitches, yarn over needle to increase, knit 2

*Repeat these 2 rows until the shawl is wide enough for you, or you've used up half your yarn.

<u>TO DECREASE:</u>

1st row: knit to end

2nd and every alt row: knit to last 5 stitches. Knit 3 together, yarn over, knit 2.

*Repeat these 2 rows until you have 5 stitches left.

Cast off.

A LITTLE IDEA...

Decorate your hair with Oak leaves!

First stabilise the tweed with interfacing before sewing to sleepie clips.

clear night stars bright

The winter I like is full of crisp frosty days, snowy walks and clear star filled nights; rosy cheeks, hot chocolate and open fires. And we mustn't forget Christmas! I love Christmas.

Winter is also the perfect season for quilters. We can just settle in by the fire with some comforting hand stitching, a little treat (to keep our strength up) and contentedly wait for spring to arrive.

Our projects this season reflect all that is good about Winter – Robins, long starry nights, wrapping up warm and the chance of a little kiss under the mistletoe!

I've often thought about designing a Christmas quilt and this year I finally have! Hopefully you'll think it's subtle enough to stay out of the loft for the whole winter and not just the twelve days. I think this quilt would be lovely with embroidered Robins too, and of course you can make your quilt as big as you like - mine is quite small.

ROBIN RED QUILT.

REQUIREMENTS:

Fabrics for nine patch blocks:
$\frac{1}{2}$ yard assorted reds
and $\frac{1}{2}$ yard calico

Fabric for appliqué blocks:
$\frac{3}{4}$ yard calico

Fabrics for the Robins appliqué:
$\frac{1}{2}$ yard

Fusible web: $\frac{1}{2}$ yard

Binding: $\frac{1}{4}$ yard

Wadding and backing fabric:
33 x 33 inches

Red sewing and quilting threads

Red embroidery threads for tying

Finished quilt measures 30 x 30 inches

INSTRUCTIONS:

1. **PREPARE:** Wash and press all the fabric. Cut twelve $6\frac{1}{2}$ x $6\frac{1}{2}$ inch squares in calico for appliqué. Cut sixty five $2\frac{1}{2}$ x $2\frac{1}{2}$ inch red squares. Cut fifty two $2\frac{1}{2}$ x $2\frac{1}{2}$ inch calico squares for nine patch blocks.

2. **NINE PATCH BLOCKS:** Chain-piece squares together to make thirteen nine patch blocks. Press.

3. **APPLIQUÉ:** Trace 12 Robins. Arrange each of them carefully in the centre of the calico squares. Press. See 'How do I?' chapter for tutorial.

4. **FREE MOTION STITCHING:** Place stabiliser behind the appliqué before free motion stitching the appliqué (see 'How do I?' chapter for tutorial).

5. **LAYER UP:** Add wadding and backing fabric.

6. **QUILT:** I machine quilted on the diagonal across the nine patch blocks and hand tied in the centre of each Robin.

7. **MAKE BINDING:** Cut 3 inch wide strips for double fold continuous binding. Stitch in place.

8. Show your quilt off to everyone - and never point out your mistakes!

I embroidered and hand quilted this
cushion one evening by the fire whilst
pretending not to watch television -
I often do that! I must say I'm
rather fond of this little Robin.

ROBIN CUSHION.

FINISHED SIZE:
Robin measures 4 x 3 inches
Cushion measures 11 inches

REQUIREMENTS:

12 x 12 inches fabric
e.g. calico for cushion front

Two 12 x 9 inches fabric
for cushion envelope back

12 x 12 inches thin wadding

Sewing and quilting threads

Red embroidery silk

Embroidery hoop

INSTRUCTIONS:

1. **PREPARE THE FABRIC:** Wash and press
   your fabric - yawn!

2. **TRACE** Robin and quilting templates
   onto fabric.

3. **ADD WADDING** behind the fabric.

4. **USE A HOOP:** Place your fabric in the hoop
   making sure it is taut enough to make a
   satisfying little 'pop' when you pull the
   needle through, but be sure not to stretch
   it out of shape.

5. **BEGIN STITCHING THE OUTLINE:** Sew with three
   strands of embroidery silk and a back stitch
   or split stitch.

6. **STITCH THE DETAILS:** Changing the thickness
   of your embroidery silk (from three to
   two strands) will add depth and texture
   to your embroidery. I only used one strand
   for the legs.

7. **QUILT:** Hand quilt the feather template
   with small stitches. Remove template lines.

8. **MAKE CUSHION:** Mine has an envelope back.

9. **SHOW OFF!** Show everyone your embroidery
   and never, ever point out your mistakes!

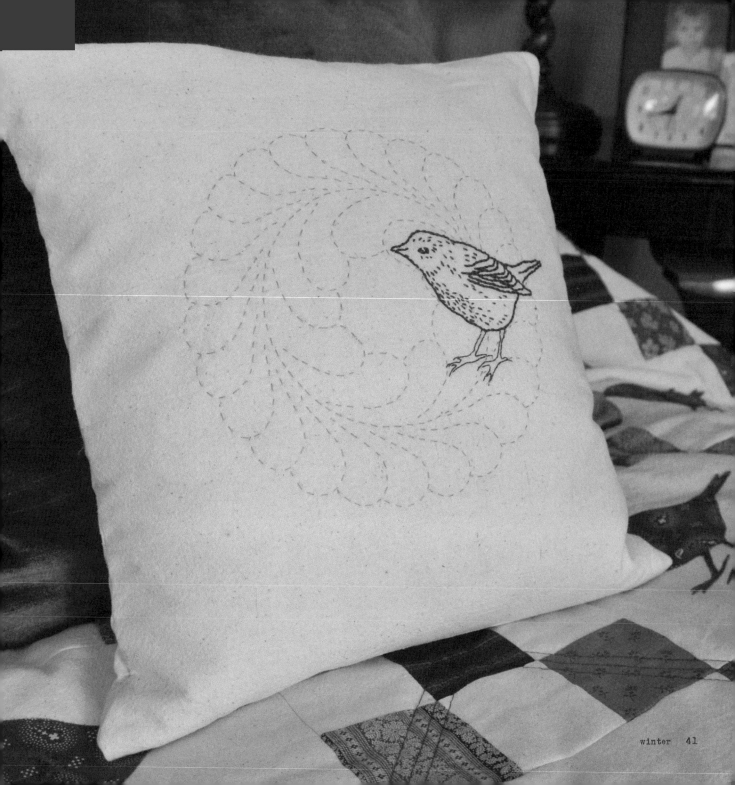

Mistletoe has such a lovely colour and shape
to it and I love its white waxy berries too.
I thought a table runner with sprigs of
embroidered mistletoe along it would look very
festive. Well, it just wouldn't be Christmas
without mistletoe would it?

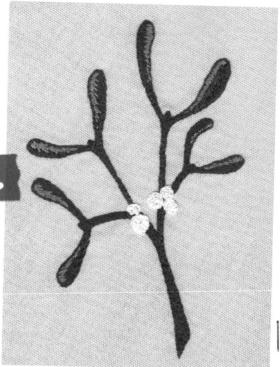

Mistletoe measures: 6 x 4 inches

MISTLETOE TABLE RUNNER.

REQUIREMENTS:
Linen fabric to fit your table,
my runner is 12 inches wide
Sewing thread
Dark and medium blue green and
white embroidery silk
Embroidery hoop

INSTRUCTIONS:

1. **PREPARE THE FABRIC**: Wash and press your fabric.

2. **MAKE TABLE RUNNER**: Make the runner to fit
   your table and hem neatly.

3. **TRACE** the large mistletoe template onto fabric.

4. **USE A HOOP**: Place your fabric in the hoop
   making sure it is taut enough to make a
   satisfying little 'pop' when you pull the
   needle through, but be sure not to stretch
   it out of shape.

5. **BEGIN STITCHING THE OUTLINE**: Sew with
   three strands of embroidery silk and a
   back stitch or split stitch.

6. **EMBROIDER**: Fill in the leaves and berries
   with a satin stitch and the different
   shades of green to add depth.

7. **SHOW OFF!** Show everyone your embroidery
   and never, ever point out your mistakes!

I actually saw a pale Owl like this one night. I was quite surprised as it flew out of the trees by the supermarket! I keep hoping to see him again, but never have. Maybe he's flown away to somewhere more pleasant - I know I would if I were him.

So, here's my pale Owl gliding on silent wings through the night sky.

WINTER

OWL IN THE NIGHT SKY.

Finished size: 15 x 10 inches

REQUIREMENTS:
20 x 15 inches wool tweed
Fabric scraps for moon and owl
Fusible web
Soluble or removable web to hand quilt through
Pale quilting thread
Metallic thread
Wood/stretcher bars, drawing pins or staples

INSTRUCTIONS:

1. PREPARE: Wash and press all the fabric. Cut background fabric to size allowing plenty of allowance for stapling to the wooden frame later.

2. APPLIQUÉ: Trace the owl and moon onto fusible web. Arrange each of them carefully and press. See 'How do I?' chapter for tutorial.

3. FREE MOTION STITCHING: Place stabiliser behind the appliqué before free motion stitching the appliqué (see 'How do I?' chapter for tutorial).

4. QUILT: Trace the feather wreaths to be quilted onto your soluble web. Position and hand quilt adding a few stitches in metallic thread too. Remove soluble web.

5. MAKE WOODEN FRAME: My wall hanging is stretched and stapled onto a simple wooden frame. Artist stretcher bars (from art shops) are ideal for this. The frame needs to measure 15 x 10 inches. Starting from the top centre pin or staple the wall hanging to the frame, turn the frame over and pin or staple at the bottom centre. Do the same at each side and then continue to stretch and pin the wall hanging to the frame, ensuring it is taut and straight.

6. SHOW YOUR WALL HANGING OFF TO EVERYONE - and never point out your mistakes!

These gloves may be the perfect
combination of warmth and practicality.
I've been known to wear them in the house
too but then my hands are always cold.

They're very simple to knit and are a
great way to use up all your odds and
ends too.

FINGERLESS GLOVES.

REQUIREMENTS:
4mm (size 8) knitting needles
Two x 50 grams double knit wool yarn
Sewing needle

INSTRUCTIONS:

1. CAST ON: On 4mm needles cast on 42st.

2. RIB: Work K2, P2 rib until work
   measures 6cm (16 rows), changing
   colour every 4 rows.

3. STOCKING STITCH: Continue in stocking
   stitch, changing colour every 4 rows
   until work measures 18cm (48 rows
   total), changing colour every 4 rows.

4. RIB: Work 4 rows in K2, P2 rib.

5. CAST OFF.

6. SEW UP. Stitch the gloves with
   right sides together leaving
   sufficient opening for the thumbs.

Make these for your favourite star gazer
- they're filled with rice and so can
be warmed in the microwave for instant
comfort. I find English paper piecing
very soothing. I know, it's slow but
where's the rush?

Of course if you can't wait you can
easily machine piece the triangles.

HEXAGONAL
HAND WARMERS.

REQUIREMENTS:
Scraps of fabric $2\frac{1}{2}$ x $2\frac{1}{2}$ inches for triangles
$4\frac{1}{2}$ x $4\frac{1}{2}$ inch fabric for backing
Sewing thread
Un-cooked rice

INSTRUCTIONS:

1. **PREPARE THE FABRIC:** Wash and press your fabric.

2. **PREPARE TEMPLATES:** Copy the larger hexagon template
   onto thin card. Use the hexagon as a template for
   the backing fabric (add seam allowance). Then cut
   the hexagon template into triangles as accurately
   as you can.

3. **CUT FABRIC:** Choose 6 different fabrics and cut
   triangles at least $\frac{1}{4}$ inch larger than the templates.

4. **TACK:** Fold fabric neatly and smoothly over each
   triangle template and tack fabric firmly in place.
   Repeat for all 6 triangles.

5. **STITCH:** Using small whip stitches with right
   sides together, stitch the first 2 triangles
   together. Continue stitching the triangles
   in place to form a hexagon.

6. **REMOVE TACKING:** Cut your tacking stitches
   out and remove the triangle templates.

7. **MAKE HAND WARMER:** Stitch front and backs together,
   leaving sufficient opening for turning right sides
   out. Fill with rice. Slipstitch opening closed.

Finished size: 8 x 4½ inches

Here's an owl for a little someone to cuddle. Are you wondering why he's called Norman? Well, it's because owls are renowned for their wisdom (sorry!)

I found some wool tweed which was perfect for him but you could always use a brushed cotton or wool felt instead.

NORMAN.

REQUIREMENTS:

18 x 10 inches wool tweed for body
24 x 4 inches wool tweed for wings
3 x inches wool tweed for face
2 buttons
Black embroidery thread
Toy stuffing

INSTRUCTIONS:

1. MAKE BODY: Trace and cut two, adding a small seam allowance.

2. SEW BODY: With right sides together, sew round the body leaving the tummy open. Turn right side out.

3. STUFF: Be careful not to over stuff (the seams will just rip if you do). Stitch tummy closed.

4. WINGS: Make two. Cut four wings adding a small seam allowance, sew right sides together, turn and slipstitch openings closed. Stitch to each side of the body with a button. Stitch points of wings together.

5. FACE: Cut one face. Embroider two eyes. Hand stitch face to the body.

A LITTLE IDEA...

Why not embroider yourself
a little reminder of your
new year's resolution?

TEMPLATE - see page 78

the beauties of nature are charming to me

Isn't that a lovely phrase?

I found it in a Shaker hymn years ago and it stayed with me. Whilst I was creating the seasonal chapters I kept thinking about nature collections and how could I actually make one in cloth, and this wall hanging is my answer.

I've used the ideas and templates scattered throughout the book, but also took the opportunity to play with rust, bleach and flower printing.

Yes, I enjoyed myself!

cold night stars bright

wisps of mist

So, now it's time
to create your very
own 'charming to you'
wall hanging.

What will yours look like?

across the land

shimmering heat

THE BEAUTIES OF NATURE.

REQUIREMENTS:

Brushed cotton fabric: 27 x 31 inches

Thin wadding: 27 x 31 inches

Fabrics, wadding scraps and threads for the appliqué blocks

1 yard cotton woven ribbon: 1 inch wide

Green embroidery thread

Fusible web: ½ yard

Wood to make frame: 23 x 27 inches

Staple gun and staples

INSTRUCTIONS:

Below are the finished sizes for the individual blocks, but I suggest you use them only as a guide. Cut your fabric by eye with scissors to help achieve a natural naïve look to the piece. Fill in any gaps with scraps of lace, buttons and favourite pieces of fabric.

14 APPLIQUÉ BLOCKS:
Flower shadow (5 x 3½ inches),
eggs (8 x 3),
bunny (4 x 3),
mistletoe (5½ x 3½),
ants (5½ x 2½),
owl (7 x 4½),
fox (6 x 5),
spider (4 x 3),
butterfly (4 x 4),
seed heads shadows (3½ x 2½),
funghi (9½ x 1½),
sycamore (4 x 3),
forget-me-not (5½ x 3)
and oak leaf (3½ x 3).

4 FREE MACHINE STITCHING BLOCKS:
Line of trees (3 x 1½),
a nettle (3 x 2½),
snail (2½ x 2) and
tiny bird (2 x 1)

3 DYED BLOCKS:
1 flower print (7 x 5),
1 rust block (6 x 4½)
and 1 bleached block (12½ x 5)

2 HAND QUILTED BLOCKS:
3½ x 2¾ inches and 4 x 4 inches

1 PAPER PIECED BLOCK: hexagon (2½)

4 EMBROIDERED PHRASES

Finished piece measures 23 x 27 inches

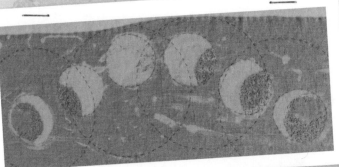

1. PREPARE: Cut background fabric to size and tea stain. Rinse and press.

2. MAKE FRAME: Or rather, get your husband to!

3. MAKE 14 APPLIQUÉ BLOCKS: Detailed instructions can be found in the 'How do I' chapter and the templates are all in the templates chapter. The blocks have wadding behind them and are also hand quilted. See Summer page 22 for instructions on making the shadow templates.

4. MAKE 3 FREE MOTION STITCHING BLOCKS: Draw a snail, a nettle and a row of trees. Follow the detailed instructions in 'How do I' for advice and tips. I also added some white French knots to the nettle.

5. MAKE RUST FABRIC: Take calico and fold it into pleats. Staple the pleats in place. Soak fabric in a solution of ½ vinegar and ½ water. Once thoroughly soaked place fabric in a plastic bag overnight or until you see the rust develop. Remove, rinse and leave to dry. Press.

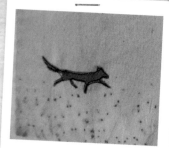

6. FLOWER PRINT: Take a fresh flower and place it between two pieces of clean ironed cloth, then take a hammer and bash the flower all over. You will see the print of the flower emerging. Remove the flower, leave the cloth to dry and iron to set colours.

7. MAKE MOON CYCLE: Draw six circles in a curve on your fabric, then using the same circle draw the segments, leaving the 3rd circle as the full moon. Dip a paintbrush in bleach and paint these areas, it doesn't matter if the cloth is splashed elsewhere. Allow the bleach to develop, and rinse when it has reached the colour you want. Iron. Using a bigger circle as a quilting template, hand quilt.

8. EMBROIDERED PHRASES: Write in a removable fabric pen 'cold night, stars bright', 'wisps of mist', 'warms the land' and 'shimmering heat', embroider using back stitch.

9. MAKE 2 QUILTING BLOCKS: Hand quilt.

10. PAPER PIECED HEXAGON: Stitch the fabric over papers. Remove papers, fold excess fabric behind and then slip stitch in place.

11. LAY OUT: Place wadding behind the background fabric. In a removable pen draw the frame on the background fabric as a guide. Arrange the blocks until you are happy and then pin in place. Needle-turn appliqué the blocks in place.

12. FRAME: Start from the top centre and staple fabric in place once. Rotate the frame, pull fabric taut and staple the bottom centre in place. Repeat for each side. Keep rotating and stapling to ensure an even result. Trim excess wadding away from the corners and fold neatly (hospital corners!), staple in place.

13. Show your quilt off to everyone - and never point out your mistakes!

HOW DO I?

I hope you are inspired to get stitching now that you have looked through my book! I'd love you to create your own designs so please adapt the patterns as you wish...

...go on, make them your own!

I love to draw with my sewing machine - and have used fusible web (Bondaweb) appliqué and free motion stitching for all the projects in the book.

Templates for almost any technique are simply line drawings, so satin stitch, needle turn or button hole your appliqué - it's your choice. Just remember that you may need to add seam allowance depending on the method you choose.

As you will have seen the instructions in the book are not much more than the order in which to do things, which is all you need if you have some experience. However, if you are a beginner there are plenty of excellent tutorials on 'You Tube' or contact your nearest quilt shop and ask about workshops. You could always come on one of mine!

So, I have concentrated here on giving good clear instructions for my fusible appliqué and free motion stitching technique.

THIS IS HOW I DO IT...

FABRIC

Rummaging through your stash and choosing
fabrics is one of the little pleasures in
life isn't it? Somehow, I seem to have a
never ending supply of scraps and as I like
to use up what I already have, most of my
quilts are scrap quilts. I often use the
reverse of a printed fabric as the right
side as it gives a lovely faded quality.
I'll use any fabric I like, be it patchwork,
dressmaking or recycled clothing. I don't
worry if it's not 100% cotton.

THREADS

I use a polyester thread because I
find it snaps and frays less easily.
I generally use just three colours:
one the colour of dust, a dark grey
and a brown. I personally, think
black thread looks too heavy.

WADDING (BATTING)

I generally use
*'Hobbs Heirloom Premium
Cotton Blend 80/20'.*

FUSIBLE WEB

I use *'Bondaweb'*.
I always use this
one because I like
the paper side for
drawing and tracing.

EMBROIDERED

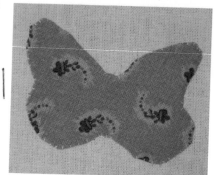

NEEDLE TURN APPLIQUÉ

FUSIBLE APPLIQUÉ &
HAND STITCHED BUTTONHOLE

FUSIBLE APPLIQUÉ &
MACHINE STITCHED BUTTONHOLE

HOW DO I?
APPLIQUÉ

1. TRACE TEMPLATES ONTO FUSIBLE WEB

You may find it easier to photocopy the templates in this book, but please do this only for your own personal use. If you want you can make them bigger or smaller too.

The templates are reversed in the book, so when they are traced and ironed onto the fabric they are facing the correct way.

The following instructions are specifically for 'Bondaweb', so please check the application instructions for your fusible web brand.

Lay a piece of Bondaweb (paper side up) over the template and trace with a sharp pencil or pen.

2. IRON TEMPLATES ONTO FABRIC

Cut the traced templates out with paper scissors leaving a small seam allowance all round. Place the templates paper side up on the reverse of your chosen fabrics.

Iron to fix in place and then cut them out as carefully as you can on your traced pencil lines.

3. POSITION APPLIQUÉ

Peel off the backing paper, if this is tricky, scratch the middle with a pin. Position all the pieces in exactly the right place before finally ironing them down on the background fabric. Be careful because they can't be moved without leaving a sticky residue on the fabric.

4. SET UP YOUR SEWING MACHINE

For most machines this means:

- Lowering the feed dogs/teeth
- Choosing the darning foot (circular or horseshoe shaped, with a spring)

My machine is happier free motion stitching if it has a new needle - I also select the needle down position, so that when I take my foot off the pedal the needle stays in the fabric and I can have a little rest without losing my place.

5. FREE MOTION STITCHING

I've said in the pattern instructions to add a stabiliser or similar behind the areas to be free motion stitched to help prevent the fabric puckering. However, I don't always do this - so see what thickness of fabric your machine is happy to stitch through nicely, you may not need it either.

Now, there's nothing else for it, you just have to start. It may end up in the bin, you may get a bobbin-y mess or a broken needle, but what does it matter?

Remember that you (and not the machine) must move the fabric and control the length of the stitches. If you were drawing with a pencil and paper, you'd move the pencil, but here you move the paper.

THINGS TO BEAR IN MIND...

LOOK WHERE YOU ARE GOING - not where you've been, it's too late for that!

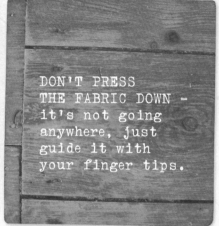

DON'T PRESS THE FABRIC DOWN - it's not going anywhere, just guide it with your finger tips.

DON'T SWIVEL THE FABRIC ROUND as you might if you were zigzagging round an appliqué, keep the fabric facing the same way at all times.

TRY NOT TO PUT YOUR FOOT TO THE FLOOR! A nice steady flowing speed is what you want.

IF YOU ARE GETTING HUNDREDS OF TINY STITCHES you are going too fast and moving the fabric too slowly.

IF YOU ARE GETTING ENORMOUS STITCHES you are going too slow and moving the fabric too fast. It really doesn't matter if all your stitches are the same length (mine certainly aren't) but the overall effect should be even.

REMEMBER that the Bondaweb has secured the appliqué to the background fabric, so your stitches are purely decorative.

LIFE IS TOO SHORT to un-pick free motion stitching. So if you can, just throw your mistakes in the bin.

Now, be nice to yourself
and have an honest look at
my stitches - they're not
all perfect either are they?

EMBROIDERY

TRACING TEMPLATES ONTO FABRIC

I use a water soluble pen to mark up embroidery or quilting patterns onto fabric. If the fabric is hard to see through when tracing hold the template and the fabric up to a window and trace them that way.

I have written instructions for my favourite stitches...

BACK STITCH

This is a very useful stitch as it forms a nice solid outline, making it perfect for embroidering words and shapes.

1.

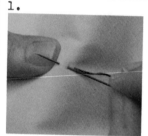

Thread the needle with 3 strands of embroidery silk. Knot one end. Come through the fabric so the knot is on the back. Stitch from right to left.

2.

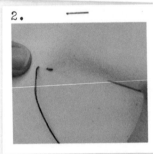

Take one stitch bringing the needle back up another stitch length away. Pull thread through so it rests on the fabric.

3.

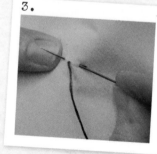

Then go backwards to meet the previous stitch, bringing the needle back up another stitch away. Continue in this way.

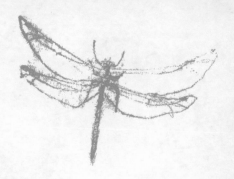

FRENCH KNOTS

These are my favourite embroidery stitches!
French Knots are literally knots which sit on top of the fabric.

1.
Start in the same way as for back stitch.

2.
Hold the embroidery thread in your left hand about an inch away from the fabric. Hold the needle horizontally to the thread.

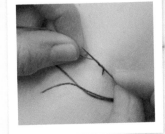

3.
Wrap the thread twice around your needle from front to back.

4.
Keeping the thread securely wrapped round the needle, push it down into the fabric, slightly above where the thread comes through in step 1.

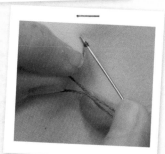

5.
Guide the thread through the fabric so it lays neatly.

6.
Finished!

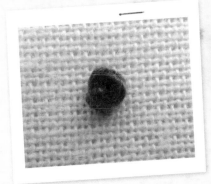

TEMPLATES

SPRING

SUMMER

AUTUMN

WINTER

BEAUTIES

every leaf

speaks bliss

● Poem Cushion

to me

fluttering from the

autumn tree

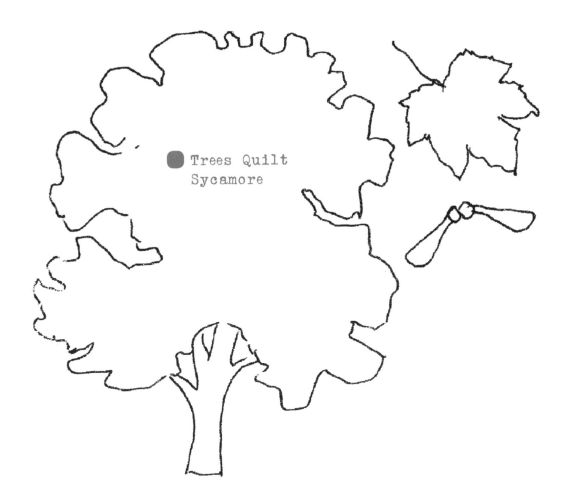

Trees Quilt
Sycamore

Rowan   Horse Chestnut

Trees Quilt

Sycamore   Oak

Trees Quilt
Rowan

Trees Quilt
Oak

TEMPLATES

SPRING
SUMMER
AUTUMN
WINTER
BEAUTIES

Trees Quilt
Horse Chestnut

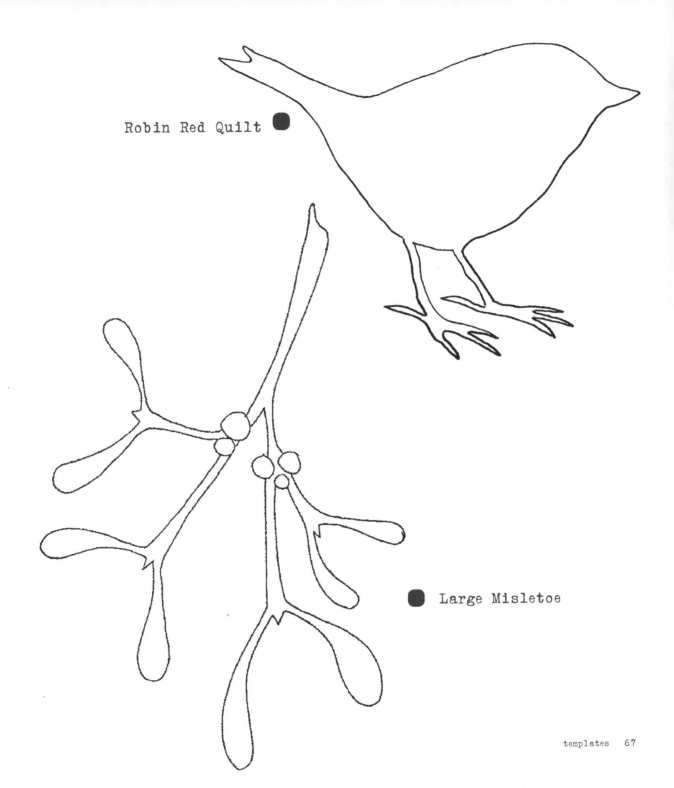

Robin Red Quilt

Large Misletoe

TEMPLATES

SPRING

SUMMER

AUTUMN

WINTER

BEAUTIES

Joys of Spring Quilt
Sweet Violet

Joys of Spring Quilt
Buttercup

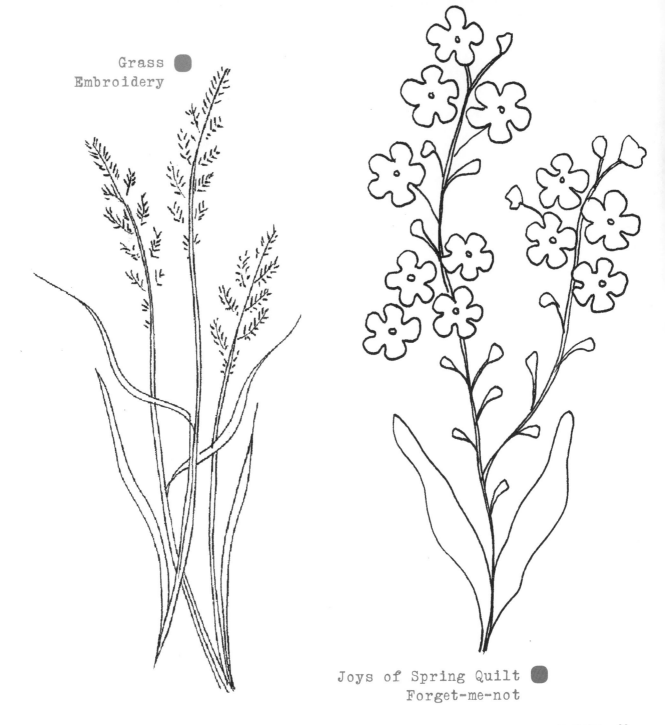

Grass
Embroidery

Joys of Spring Quilt
Forget-me-not

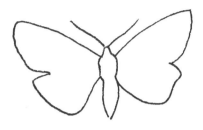

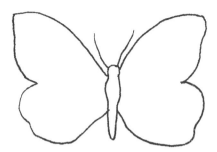

Butterflies &
Bugs Quilt

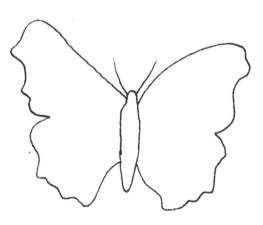

Pieces of Song Cushion
Blackbird

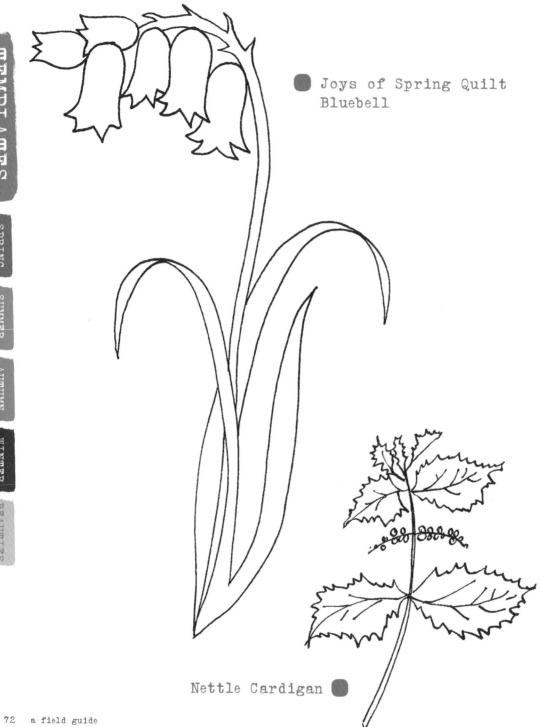

TEMPLATES

SPRING
SUMMER
AUTUMN
WINTER
BEAUTIES

Joys of Spring Quilt
Bluebell

Nettle Cardigan

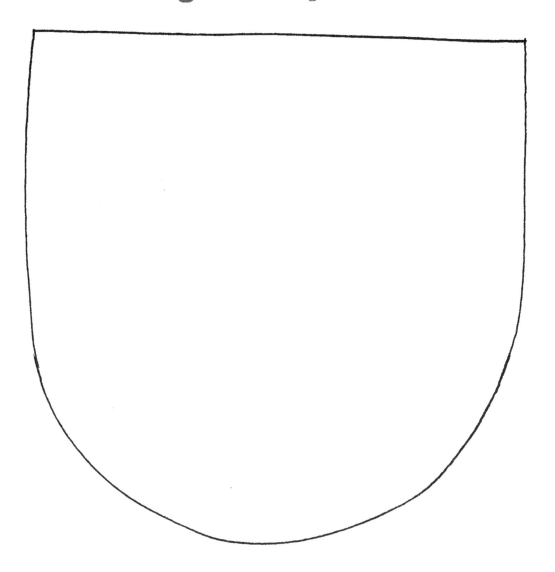

Nettle Cardigan Pocket

Owl Night Sky
Quilting

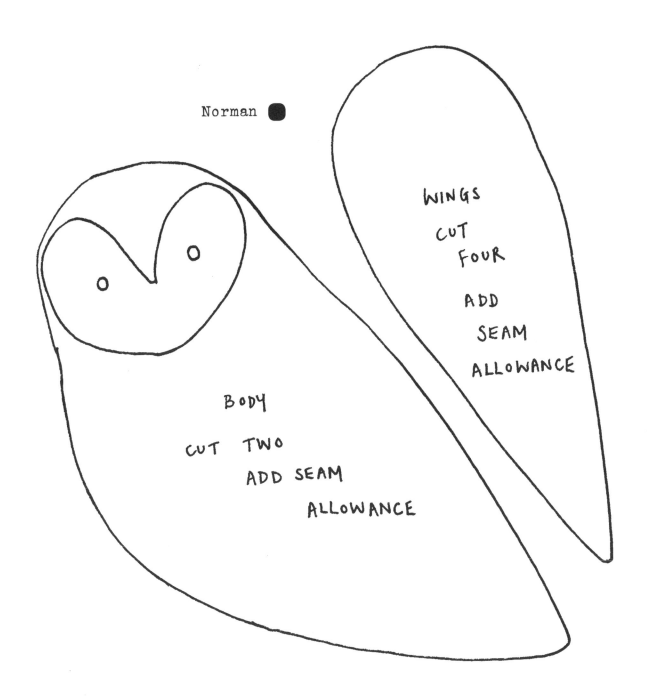

Norman

WINGS
CUT
FOUR
ADD
SEAM
ALLOWANCE

BODY
CUT TWO
ADD SEAM
ALLOWANCE

Robin Cushion
Embroidery

Joys of Spring
Quilting

Bunnies Appliqué

Hexagonal
Handwarmer
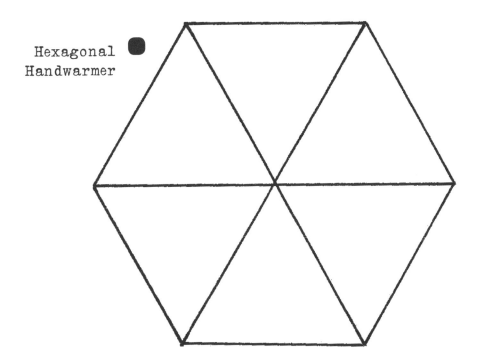

SPRING
SUMMER
AUTUMN
WINTER
BEAUTIES

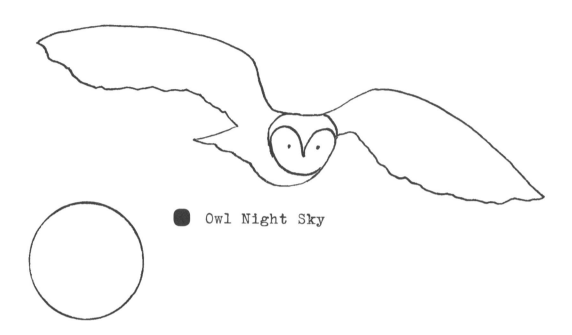

● Owl Night Sky

Slow down ● Little idea

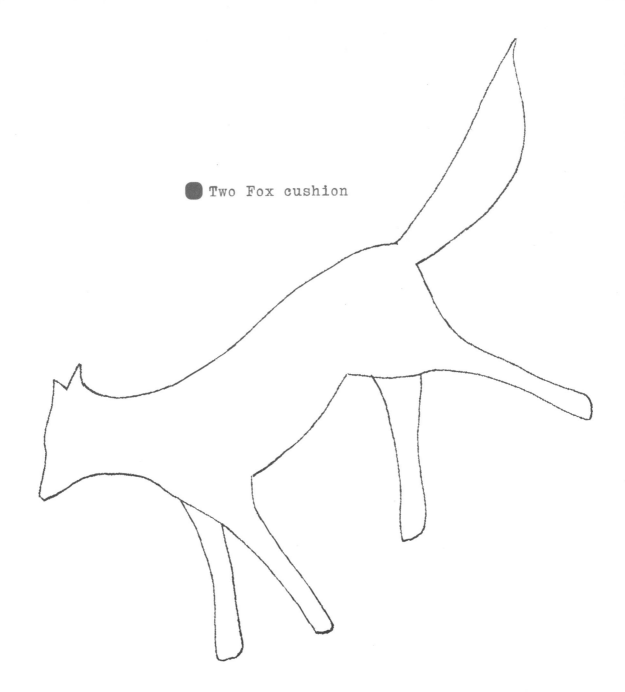

● Two Fox cushion

INDEX

Here's my little guide to help you find the right page...

wasps of mist

Shimmering heat

YOUR FIELD NOTES...

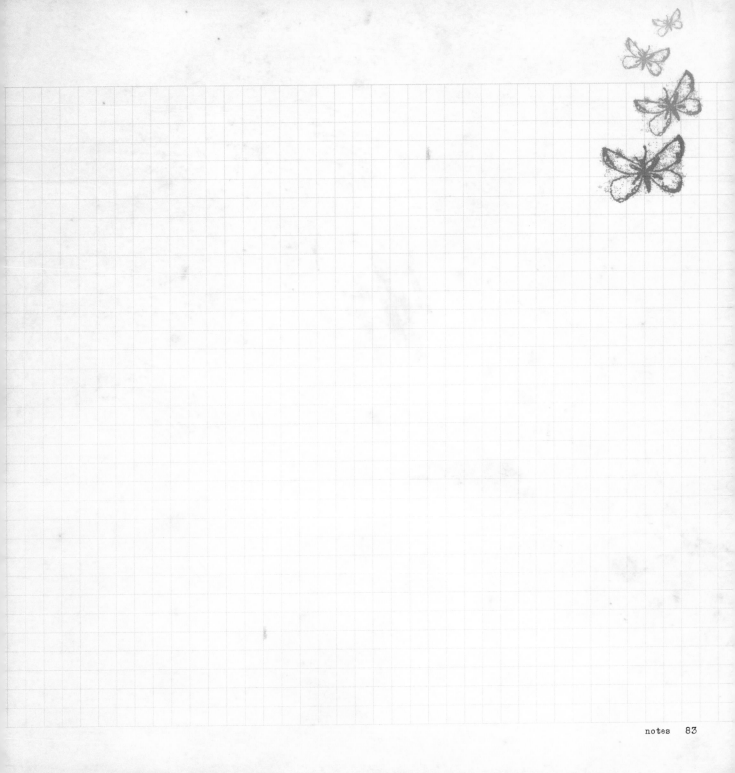

YOUR FIELD NOTES...

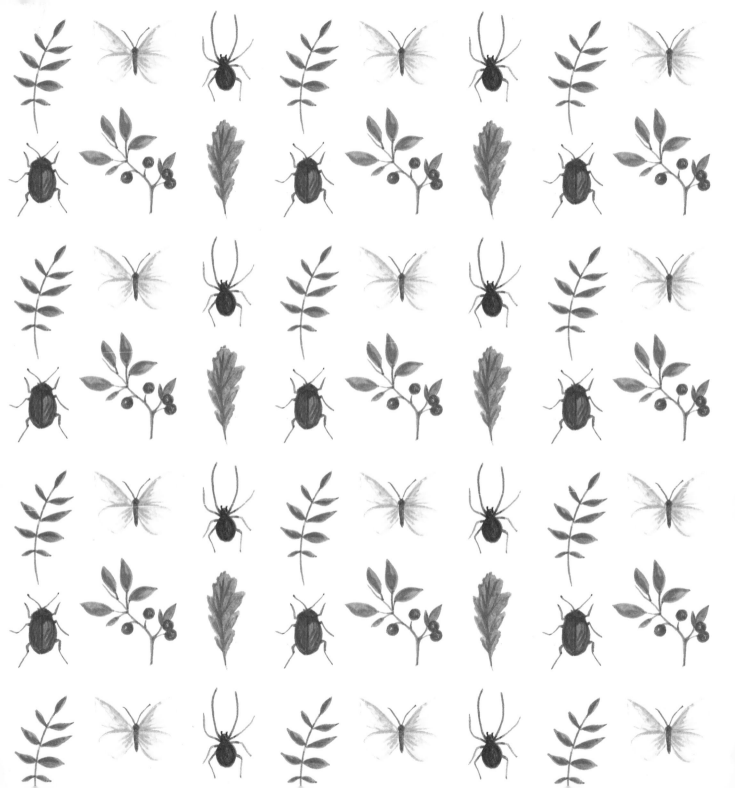